CW01512632

Original title:

Lavender Rays Inside the Spider Copse

Author: Aron Pilviste

ISBN HARDBACK: 978-1-80559-084-2

ISBN PAPERBACK: 978-1-80559-583-0

The Choreography of the Veiled World

In shadows dance, the whispers weave,
A tapestry where dreams believe.
Calming echoes, secrets hum,
In twilight's pulse, the night will come.

Figures merge in graceful flow,
Veils of silence softly glow.
Beneath the stars, old legends swell,
In every shadow, stories dwell.

The moon's embrace, a guiding hand,
With every sway, we understand.
Threads of fate in silken ties,
As time unveils the night's disguise.

A quiet ballet, spirits twirl,
In the stillness of the world.
Hearts entwined in unseen chains,
In gentle movements, love remains.

As dawn approaches, shadows fade,
Yet in our souls, the dance is laid.
For in the veils of life we find,
The choreography of the mind.

Enclaves of Color in Dusk's Reach

Amidst the hues, the sunlight spills,
A canvas brushed with nature's thrills.
Where oranges spark and violets blend,
In dusk's embrace, horizons bend.

Golden rays in shadows collide,
Whispers of light where dreams abide.
Blooming echoes in twilight's song,
In colors deep, we all belong.

Crimson skies as day departs,
Painted strokes on gentle hearts.
In enclaves where soft colors play,
Dusk unveils the end of day.

Embers flicker, stars awake,
In silent shades, our passions shake.
Each brush of dusk, a sweet caress,
In vibrant rhythms, we find rest.

As night descends, the palette shifts,
Upon our souls, the darkness lifts.
In every shade, a hidden peace,
Dusk's colors hold our sweet release.

Whispers of Violet Twilight

In twilight's embrace, colors blend,
Violet whispers, messages send.
A gentle breeze stirs the leaves,
Where time slows down, and magic weaves.

The stars peep out, shy and meek,
Painting the night with a subtle streak.
Dreams take flight on the moon's soft glow,
In this tranquil hour, secrets flow.

Silent echoes of the fading light,
Kissing the world, soft as a sigh.
Each heartbeat sings a soulful tune,
Under the watch of a wistful moon.

Violet hues dress the evening sky,
Telling tales where shadows lie.
In stillness, hearts begin to yearn,
For the nights when the stars return.

As the night unfolds its tender wings,
Love and hope are the songs it sings.
Find your place in the violet mist,
In every whisper, a dream exists.

Secrets Among the Weaving Shadows

Among the trees, shadows dance,
Silent secrets, a fleeting chance.
Whispers of light fade away,
As twilight beckons the end of day.

Beneath the boughs, stories dwell,
In every rustle, a hidden spell.
The moonlight casts intricate lines,
Weaving tales where the heart entwines.

Footsteps linger on the soft ground,
In the stillness, truth is found.
Shadows mingle, soft and gray,
Guarding secrets that wish to stay.

A breeze carries echoes of the past,
In its embrace, memories last.
Each leaf a page in nature's book,
Inviting the curious, come take a look.

Among the dark, light starts to gleam,
Echoing softly like a forgotten dream.
Secrets unfold in the soft night air,
Weaving stories for those who dare.

A Dance of Purple Dreams

In realms where colors softly blend,
A waltz of dreams begins to send.
Purple hues in the dusky sky,
Whispering softly as they fly.

Stars begin their graceful dance,
Inviting the dreamers with a glance.
Twinkling tales of love and light,
Filling the heart with such delight.

In the garden where wishes bloom,
Petals whisper in the moonlit gloom.
Each moment glimmers, sweet and rare,
A treasure to find in the evening air.

As melodies drift on the evening breeze,
The world holds its breath, time seems to freeze.
Dreams entwined in the night's embrace,
A dance of joy, a sacred space.

From dusk till dawn, the dreams will soar,
Carried on wings to forevermore.
In this twilight, let your heart gleam,
And sway with the rhythm of purple dreams.

Enchantment in the Sylvan Web

In shadows deep, enchantment brews,
The sylvan web, where magic cues.
Sunlight filters through the leaves,
Drawing whispers, the forest weaves.

The brook hums softly, tales of old,
Every ripple, a story told.
In twilight's grasp, the air is sweet,
Where earth and stars gracefully meet.

Creatures flit in the quiet night,
Dancing with shadows, pure delight.
Mossy paths, where echoes blend,
Lead to secrets that nature sends.

With every breeze, the night unfolds,
In hues of deep and bright marigolds.
A tapestry spun by unseen hands,
Holding the dreams of distant lands.

So linger here in the shaded light,
Among the wonders, pure and bright.
For in the heart of this sylvan web,
Lies endless magic, an eternal ebb.

Echoes of the Enchanted Silks

In the shadows, whispers weave,
Colors dance as hearts believe.
Threads of magic, silent call,
Binding dreams that never fall.

Moonlight glimmers on the thread,
Stories linger, softly said.
Each stitch carries tales of old,
Crafted treasures of the bold.

Fingers trace the fabric's grace,
Every fold, a warm embrace.
Breathless secrets wrapped in hue,
Echoes linger, softly true.

As the night wraps round the loom,
Fate unveils its mystic bloom.
From the fibers, voices rise,
Echoes whisper, never guise.

In enchanted silks, we find,
Hearts entwined, forever blind.
Woven moments, sacred art,
Threads of love, a beating heart.

Whispers Beneath the Latticed Veil

Softly sighs the evening breeze,
Beneath the veil of whispering leaves.
Secrets linger, shadows play,
In the dusk, hope finds its way.

Latticed skies of twilight's grace,
Dreams unfold in this safe space.
With each breath, the darkness hums,
A promise kept, as daylight succumbs.

Stars emerge, a gentle choir,
Lighting paths with soft desire.
Underneath this woven charm,
Whispers rise, a soothing balm.

In the corners, shadows creep,
While the world around us sleeps.
Beneath the lattice, hearts align,
In the whispers, love will shine.

Underneath the silken night,
Veils of calm, a tender sight.
In the stillness, spirits soar,
Whispers linger evermore.

The Scent of Twilight's Gift

When twilight falls, the colors blend,
A fragrant breeze, our senses tend.
The world transforms in softer light,
As whispers dance in the embrace of night.

Petals open, secrets unfold,
With every hue, a tale is told.
Lavender dreams in twilight's breath,
Scent of magic, love, and death.

In the dusk, a promise sweet,
Nature weaves a rhythmic beat.
With twilight's gift, hearts awaken,
In its aroma, bonds unshaken.

As shadows stretch and silence grows,
The fragrance deepens, softly flows.
With every sigh, the dark adorns,
The scent of magic, new love born.

From the dusk, a lingering trace,
Twilight's gift, a warm embrace.
In every heart, the whispers cling,
Scent of twilight, eternal spring.

Dappled Dreams in Shade

In the garden, sunlight weaves,
Dappled dreams where nature leaves.
Softly filtered, light's warm hand,
Shadows dance across the land.

Underneath the willow's sway,
Whispers beckon, come and play.
Leaves a rustle, secrets shared,
In this space, hearts are bared.

Violet blooms and emerald green,
Nature's canvas, softly seen.
In the stillness, dreams ignite,
Woven tales in the fading light.

A tapestry of colors flow,
In the shade, our spirits grow.
Each step taken in the glade,
Finds a place where love is made.

As the day begins to wane,
Dappled dreams remain the same.
In the quiet, hope is laid,
In the heartbeat of the shade.

Silken Paths Underneath the Sky

Beneath the stars, the wanderer glides,
Soft whispers of night, where freedom resides.
Moonlight dances on the silken way,
Guiding dreams till the break of day.

Shadows play gently on the ground,
Footsteps echo with a muffled sound.
Each twist and turn, a story unfolds,
In the heart of the night, the world beholds.

The breeze carries tales from afar,
Of ancient secrets and the wishes they spar.
With every breath, the journey ignites,
As silken paths twinkle in the moon's light.

Whispers of winds caress the trees,
Rustling leaves keep their mysteries.
Nature's embrace, a comforting sway,
Underneath the sky, the soul finds its way.

So journey on through night's gentle grace,
Embracing the magic held in this space.
For silken paths weave in endless flow,
A tapestry woven, where dreams brightly glow.

Hues of Night Weaving Through the Trees

In the cloak of dusk, colors entwine,
Deep indigos kiss the forest line.
Silver branches stretch toward the moon,
Hues of night hum a soft, sweet tune.

Crickets chirp in the velvet night,
While owls hoot with wisdom and might.
Each shade a whisper, each hue a tale,
As night reveals its wondrous veil.

Stars flicker gently, like candle flames,
Painting the sky with silent claims.
Within the woods, shadows gently play,
Where dreams and reality softly sway.

Misty veils drape the ground below,
Grounding us in the night's gentle flow.
Through emerald leaves, the mystery gleams,
As darkness swells with enchanted dreams.

So come, step softly, let your heart see,
The hues of night are wild and free.
Together we roam under tree and star,
In Nature's embrace, we wander far.

The Veil of Violet in the Thicket

In the thicket where violets bloom,
A delicate beauty dispels the gloom.
Petals whisper secrets caught in the air,
Inviting all wanderers to linger and stare.

Soft twilight seeps through each green bough,
A veil of violet coats nature's brow.
With every breath, enchantment grows,
As twilight's kiss on the petals glows.

Amidst the thorns, peace finds its way,
A hidden garden where shadows sway.
Each flower a story, each leaf a rhyme,
In violet veils, we travel through time.

The fragrance pulls us deeper still,
Where silence reigns and hearts are filled.
A sanctuary nestled, soft and sweet,
In the thicket, wonder and magic meet.

So pause in the thicket, let your thoughts fly,
Embrace the beauty beneath the sky.
For in the veil of violet's embrace,
Lives a moment, a stillness, a sacred space.

Nature's Tapestry of Enchantment

Threads of color weave through the trees,
Gentle strokes carried on the breeze.
Nature's canvas, a painting alive,
In every petal, the wonders thrive.

Golden rays pour through the leaves,
While the heart of the forest softly believes.
Each rustle a note in a melodic song,
Embracing the wild where all souls belong.

Whispers of magic in every sound,
In Nature's weave, pure peace is found.
With each step, the ground pulses a beat,
In this tapestry warm, we find our retreat.

The colors fade softly as day turns to night,
Stars dot the sky, a celestial sight.
In the quiet of dusk, let your spirit soar,
For Nature's enchantment forever restores.

So linger a moment, let spirit flow,
Through winding paths where all wonders grow.
In Nature's embrace, we find our way,
A tapestry woven with dreams that won't fray.

Lullabies of the Spider's Sanctuary

In corners where shadows dance and play,
The spider weaves dreams in silken sway.
Each thread a whisper, soft and light,
Lullabies echo through the night.

With gentle hands, the night unfolds,
Stories of warmth, secrets untold.
Crickets join in, a symphony sweet,
While the moonlight wraps the world in a sheet.

Beneath the stars, the web aglow,
A fragile kingdom where soft winds blow.
Nature's wonders, a silent art,
Binding the night with a tender heart.

In this haven, the world's at ease,
Safety found in the whispering breeze.
Close your eyes, let the dreams take flight,
In lullabies spun by the spider at night.

The world outside begins to fade,
As the heart finds peace in the arachnid's braid.
Drift away in a gossamer sea,
In the sanctuary where the soul roams free.

Stretched Silhouettes of the Night

Beneath the cloak of a velvet sky,
Whispers of shadows linger and sigh.
Silhouettes stretch, merging with stars,
A canvas painted with silent memoirs.

The world in tones of deep indigo,
Dreams tread lightly, silent and slow.
Figures dance in the moon's embrace,
Every shape holds a secret place.

In twilight's glow, the stars ignite,
Drawing paths across the vast night.
Soft beams illuminate the unknown,
Guiding lost souls to find their own.

Night's canvas weaves tales untold,
Of love and longing, soft and bold.
Every shadow a fleeting glance,
In the dark, the heart finds its dance.

So let us wander, hand in hand,
Through this kingdom of starlit sand.
Where stretched silhouettes of the night,
Invite us to dream till the morning light.

Echoes of Enigmatic Blossoms

In gardens where secrets intertwine,
Blooms whisper stories in fragrant design.
Petals unfold like pages turned,
Echoes of wisdom, patiently yearned.

Every flower dons a unique hue,
Tales of the sun and the morning dew.
Winds carry scents, memories run deep,
Among enigmatic blossoms that sleep.

Sunrise awakens the vibrant spree,
As colors burst forth, wild and free.
Butterflies flutter, a dance in the air,
Completing the picture with delicate care.

Old roots entwined in the soft earth's heart,
Nurturing dreams, where life gets its start.
In silence, they bloom, without a sound,
Echoes of beauty in abundance found.

So pause a moment, in gardens vast,
To hear the echoes of a love that lasts.
In every blossom, a world to explore,
Enigmatic whispers forevermore.

In Shadows Drenched in Softness

In the folds of dusk, where light turns meek,
Shadows embrace with a tender cheek.
A gentle hush blankets the earth,
Cradling whispers of twilight's birth.

Underneath the stars, silence holds tight,
Dreams take form, cloaked in the night.
Softly they drift, like feathers in flight,
Guided by starlight, pure and bright.

Embraced by darkness, a calm retreat,
Echoes of solace in every heartbeat.
In these shadows, secrets arise,
Cocooned in softness, beneath the skies.

Every flicker, a story untold,
Wrapped in comfort, warm yet bold.
In shadows draped, find your grace,
Where the heart can linger in a sacred space.

So let your soul dance in the night,
Unravel your dreams, take gentle flight.
In shadows drenched in softness, rejoice,
For here in the dark, we find our voice.

Mysteries Entwined in Silent Corners

Whispers weave through shadows deep,
In corners where secrets sleep.
Veils of dusk conceal the truth,
Echoes of forgotten youth.

Starlit eyes and hidden sighs,
Life in stillness softly lies.
Threads of fate in silence twine,
Mysteries lost, yet to find.

Crickets chirp a solemn tune,
Underneath the silver moon.
Leaves rustle with tales they know,
In the night where wild dreams grow.

Between the walls of time and space,
We uncover the hidden trace.
Glimmers of hope in quiet air,
All that lingers, everywhere.

Softly now, the twilight calls,
As shadows dance and daylight falls.
In silent corners, stories lie,
Awaiting hearts that dare to pry.

Shadows Adorned with Amethyst Light

In the dusk where shadows blend,
Amethyst hues around me send.
Glimmers dance upon the ground,
Whispers soft and dreams unbound.

Moonlit paths and gentle sighs,
Echoes of the evening sky.
Mystic shades softly sway,
Guiding souls who've lost their way.

Through the night, a tale unfolds,
Of longing hearts and secrets told.
Stars adorn this quiet night,
Underneath the amethyst light.

Every shadow holds a spark,
Dreams ignited in the dark.
With each breath, the night takes flight,
In embrace of ethereal light.

Here where time and space entwine,
In shadows, true meanings shine.
We gather moments, soft and bright,
In the glow of the amethyst light.

The Spider's Lullaby in the Dusk

In the twilight, webs are spun,
A lullaby when day is done.
Gentle threads in silence sway,
Nature's song of night and play.

The spider weaves in shadows tight,
Cradling dreams in fading light.
Each stitch a tale, each knot a sigh,
Whispers of the night that fly.

Concealed beneath the crescent moon,
Life emerges, crickets croon.
With every pulse, the dance unfolds,
Stories spun in silken folds.

Twilight wraps the world so snug,
In the web, a tranquil hug.
Stillness hums a sweet refrain,
A lullaby to ease the pain.

As the stars begin to gleam,
Spider dreams weave through the stream.
In the dusk, all hearts align,
With the spider's lullaby divine.

Twilight's Embrace in the Woodland

In the forest where shadows play,
Twilight whispers, ending day.
Leaves cascade with colors bright,
Embracing softly, the coming night.

Gentle breezes weave through trees,
Carrying the scent of ease.
Nature's canvas, rich and bold,
Stories of the earth retold.

Sunset glows with amber charms,
Wrapping woods in tender arms.
Every creature finds its place,
In twilight's warm and loving grace.

As shadows lengthen, peace blooms wide,
In the woodland's gentle tide.
Stars awaken, one by one,
In the embrace of night begun.

Here we gather, hearts aligned,
In the stillness, love we find.
Twilight's magic fills the air,
A quiet promise, a whispered prayer.

The Fable of Glistening Canopies

In the woods where sunlight drips,
Leaves glitter like a painter's brush.
Nature hums in soft whispers,
While the gentle breeze makes a hush.

Birds weave tales of flight and song,
Through branches where the light does play.
Their melodies dance all around,
In this realm where shadows sway.

Underneath the vibrant dome,
Moss carpets the ground with care.
A secret world is softly formed,
In the canopies, wild and rare.

Mirrored pools reflect the sky,
As dragonflies flicker and dart.
Each ripple tells a fleeting tale,
Of glistening magic, nature's art.

The fable lives within each leaf,
A testament to life's grand weave.
In glistening canopies we find,
The peace that hearts shall ever seek.

In Purlieu of Shimmering Shadows

In twilight's arms, shadows dance,
Where whispers float on the air.
Lost in dreams, we take a chance,
In purlieu's realm, without a care.

Moonlight spills on the forest floor,
Painting whispers of silver hue.
Each glimmer speaks of tales of yore,
Where the night reveals the new.

Silhouettes linger in the night,
Beneath the watchful starry dome.
In shimmering shadows, taking flight,
We find our hearts, we find our home.

Faint echoes of footfalls roam,
Tracing paths where mysteries lie.
In the stillness, spirits comb,
The secrets of the night sky's sigh.

A world awash with dreams untold,
Where every breath a story spins.
In shimmering shadows, brave and bold,
Our journey of wonder begins.

Secrets of the Hidden Glimmers

Hidden glimmers beneath the boughs,
Waiting silent, shyly bright.
In the stillness, nature bows,
To secrets cloaked in soft twilight.

Each fern and flower knows the way,
To keep their treasures held secure.
In the silence, they softly play,
As the heart learns to endure.

Whispers of the ancient trees,
Echo softly, old and wise.
They share tales with the gentle breeze,
Of hidden glimmers, where magic lies.

Underneath, the earth's embrace,
A world of wonder, quaint and rare.
In stillness, we may find our place,
Amongst the glimmers, beyond compare.

The secrets dwell, forever kept,
In nature's heart, an endless song.
With each step, we have leapt,
Into glimmers where we belong.

The Golden Hour's Silken Refuge

As day bids night a soft goodbye,
The sun drapes gold on every leaf.
In this hour, the heart can fly,
Finding solace, sweet relief.

Shadows stretch and colors blend,
Painting skies in pastel hues.
Light weaves stories that won't end,
In glowing warmth, the soul renews.

A refuge found where silence reigns,
And time drips slowly like warm honey.
In golden hour, joy sustains,
With every glance, the world feels funny.

The horizon blushes with delight,
As twilight approaches, calm and fair.
In this moment, everything's right,
The day's embrace, a soft affair.

Nestled in this silken glow,
Worries fade like mist at dawn.
In golden hour, we come to know,
The beauty of a world reborn.

Testament of the Diaphanous Weave

In shadows soft, the stories lie,
A tapestry of dreams that sigh.
Each thread a whisper, light as air,
We dance in silence, unaware.

Through strands of hope, our fates entwine,
A delicate touch, both yours and mine.
We spin our tales in twilight's glow,
In this diaphanous weave, we flow.

With every thread, a heartbeat's song,
We find our place where we belong.
Embroidered secrets, hidden deep,
In memory's arms, we gently sleep.

The loom of life, it sways and bends,
As time unravels, and silence mends.
With nimble fingers, we create,
A testament of love and fate.

So let us weave with care and grace,
Each vibrant hue, a warm embrace.
In this grand design, we leave our mark,
A shining thread within the dark.

Alchemy of Twilight's Embrace

As day retreats, the night unfolds,
In twilight's arms, our dreams are told.
The stars appear, like whispers kind,
A magic dance of heart and mind.

We blend our thoughts in colors bright,
An alchemy of shadow and light.
In every glance, a spark ignites,
The promise held in whispered nights.

With gentle hands, we craft our fate,
In darkness found, we celebrate.
The moonlight casts a silver hue,
In twilight's realm, it's me and you.

From dusk to dawn, we weave and spin,
An endless cycle, where all begins.
In shadows deep, our secrets dwell,
A love like this, we know so well.

So let us share this twilight kiss,
An alchemy of bitter and bliss.
In every moment, let us find,
The beauty forged in heart and mind.

Memory Threads in a Silken Labyrinth

In winding paths where memories weave,
A silken labyrinth, we believe.
Each corner turned, a story speaks,
In quiet echoes, the heart seeks.

Through golden threads of joy and pain,
We trace the joys, we bear the stain.
In knots of time, our lives entwine,
A tapestry that's both yours and mine.

With fragile strands, we map our dreams,
In whispered truths, our essence gleams.
A dance of shadows, light and dark,
In this maze of love, we leave our mark.

Through every twist, a lesson learned,
With every turn, new passions burned.
In this labyrinth, we find our grace,
Where every thread knows its place.

So let us wander, hand in hand,
Through this silken wonderland.
In every step, a moment's bliss,
In memory's weave, we find our kiss.

The Harmony of the Dusky Light

In dusky light, our souls take flight,
A harmony, soft and bright.
With every glance, the world takes pause,
In gentle whispers, love's sweet cause.

As colors blend, the shadows play,
A symphony for end of day.
In twilight's hands, we find our song,
A melody where we belong.

With every heartbeat, rhythms swell,
In dusky hues, our stories tell.
Each note a spark of love's embrace,
In harmony, we find our place.

As night descends, our spirits soar,
In laughter shared, we seek for more.
With open hearts, we journey dare,
In dusky light, our dreams laid bare.

So let us dance beneath the stars,
In symphonies of who we are.
In harmony, we'll chase the night,
Forever bound in dusky light.

A Symphony of Sombre Floral Whispers

In gardens where shadows weave,
Petals sigh in twilight's embrace.
Their secrets, like whispers, grieve,
A symphony of lost time's trace.

Beneath the veil of silent dew,
Each blossom tells a tale of woe.
In colors dimmed, yet striking hue,
They dance where fading breezes blow.

The air is thick with fragrant tears,
As mourning winds through petals glide.
With every note, the heart adheres,
To melodies in silence bide.

In twilight's grip, the flowers bloom,
Their gentle faces speak of night.
Amidst the gloom, they cast their doom,
A chorus lost to fickle light.

Yet in this sorrow, beauty lies,
Each petal whispers soft goodbyes.
In every fade, a new sunrise,
Awakens dreams where shadows rise.

Beneath the Canopy of Gentle Echoes

Underneath the ancient trees,
A world awakens, soft and slow.
Whispers weave like fragrant breeze,
In harmony, they ebb and flow.

The leaves converse in rustling tones,
A lullaby of nature's lore.
Branches cradle hidden stones,
Where echoes linger evermore.

Moss carpets earth with muted grace,
Each step a symphony of sound.
Beneath the stars, in this safe space,
Peace envelops, softly found.

The nightingale sings sweet refrain,
While shadows twirl in soft arcs.
Each echo holds a hint of pain,
Yet beauty glistens, like the sparks.

In solace found beneath the glow,
Of moonlit secrets best kept tight,
The canopy spins tales to sow,
Of gentle echoes through the night.

Starlight and Silk in Mystical Harmony

In twilight's clutch, where starlight winks,
Silken threads weave dreams anew.
Gentle whispers dance, and links,
The cosmos hums a tune so true.

The moon spills silver on the glade,
Where shadows twine, they twist and play.
Each sparkle glimmers, softly laid,
A tapestry of night's ballet.

Flowers bloom with radiant grace,
Bathed in shimmer, soft and round.
Their colors merge in swift embrace,
A harmony where love is found.

As night descends, the world retreats,
Into a hush of velvet dark.
In every corner, silence greets,
Where starlight sings its gentle arc.

Within this dance of silk and light,
Mystical dreams begin to soar.
Lost in the magic of the night,
Hearts entwined, forevermore.

Moonlit Dreams Among the Twisted Branches

Among the limbs of gnarled oak,
Secrets lie in shadows cast.
The moon weaves tales with every stroke,
Of time that stirs both slow and fast.

Dreams whisper through the twist and turns,
Carried on the night's cool breath.
In every flicker, longing yearns,
For solace found beyond sweet death.

The branches cradle midnight's grace,
Their forms a maze of dark and light.
In this embrace, I seek a place,
Where fears dissolve and dreams take flight.

Stars flicker like forgotten thoughts,
Illuminating paths once lost.
Among the leaves, my heart is caught,
Awake, yet haunted by the cost.

In moonlit silence, shadows play,
A symphony of soft goodbyes.
Among these roots, I choose to stay,
And weave my dreams where beauty lies.

Fragments of a Dreamt Horizon

In whispers of twilight's glow,
Shadows dance where dreams flow.
Stars blink in a velvet sky,
Wishes soar, then softly sigh.

The world fades in a gentle hush,
Time stands still, a fleeting rush.
Threads of light weave through the dark,
Chasing echoes, kindled spark.

Mountains rise like silent ghosts,
Guarding tales of ancient hosts.
A river's song, sweet and clear,
Carries hopes, dispelling fear.

Softly glimmer the realms unseen,
Where hearts blend with shades of green.
Each heartbeat, a fleeting trace,
Of love's dance in a sacred space.

As dawn breaks the dream's soft dome,
Awakening a sense of home.
Fragments whisper stories wide,
In the light where dreams abide.

Embraced by the Gentle Mists

In quiet morn, the world awakes,
Wrapped in mists like soft lake breaks.
Whispers float on the chilly air,
Nature sighs in tender care.

Veils of gray through trees entwine,
Every step feels pure divine.
The sun peeks through, a golden ray,
Chasing shadows, urging play.

Ferns unfurl in emerald grace,
Life blooms slow in this sacred space.
Each breath a bond, serene and light,
In the embrace of morning's might.

Birdsong weaves a gentle thread,
Inviting dreams where hearts are led.
Drifting clouds in tender sway,
Guide the soul along the way.

With each step, the world expands,
Nature's pulse in fragile hands.
Embraced by mists, we find our place,
In harmony, a sweet embrace.

A Canvas of Hushed Mirage

Beneath the skies, a canvas bright,
Colors blend in soft twilight.
Brush strokes of forgotten lore,
Paint the dreams that we explore.

Waves of sand and whispers low,
Tales of old begin to flow.
Every grain, a moment caught,
In the silence, wisdom sought.

A mirage dances, flickers near,
Inviting all to draw it near.
Reflections of a world undone,
Chasing echoes of the sun.

In twilight's grasp, the heart will soar,
Imagining what lies in store.
With every brush, a story shared,
A canvas bright, our souls laid bare.

Hushed mirage in twilight's gleam,
Awakens yet another dream.
Painted skies hold secrets vast,
A promise of the future cast.

Echoes in the Verdant Abyss

In depths where silence reigns supreme,
Nature hums a timeless theme.
Leaves dance gently, rivers sigh,
In the abyss where spirits fly.

Mossy stones and shaded light,
Guard the secrets of the night.
Whispers echo in the green,
Of forgotten loves, and dreams unseen.

With each step, the stories grow,
In every breeze, a tale to show.
Hidden paths lead us away,
Into realms where shadows play.

Fiona's song emerges clear,
Calling forth what we hold dear.
In verdant depths, the heart finds peace,
A moment's joy, a sweet release.

As stars awaken, night descends,
The cycle shifts, the journey bends.
Echoes linger, softly kissed,
In the abyss, we coexist.

Whispers of Indigo Light

In the stillness of the night,
Whispers float, a soft delight.
Beneath the stars, dreams take flight,
Wrapped in shades of indigo light.

Gentle breezes weave and sway,
Carrying secrets to the bay.
Moonlit paths where spirits play,
In shadows deep, hearts find their way.

Echoes dance upon the breeze,
Rays of hope among the trees.
Each soft murmur, heart agrees,
In dreams alive, we find our peace.

A tapestry of night unfolds,
Tales of love and life retold.
With each whisper, magic molds,
In indigo light, the heart beholds.

As dawn approaches, shadows fade,
Yet in our hearts, the song is made.
Whispers linger, never laid,
In the light, our dreams displayed.

Beneath the Gossamer Canopy

Beneath the leaves, a world concealed,
Whispers and wonders, softly revealed.
Sunbeams filter through the trees,
In the breeze, a gentle tease.

Fluttering wings, a dance so bright,
Nature's secrets in morning light.
Petals unfurl, colors collide,
In this haven where dreams reside.

Shadows play on the emerald ground,
Every heartbeat, a joyous sound.
Voices of nature, a joyous choir,
In this grove, our souls aspire.

Gossamer threads of silver spun,
Twinkling softly as day is done.
Laughter echoed, pure and free,
In the canopy, we find decree.

As twilight descends, a hush falls low,
Stars awaken, softly aglow.
Beneath this veil, we make our plea,
In nature's arms, home we shall be.

Secrets of the Twilight Grove

In the twilight, shadows blend,
Where time whispers, and dreams descend.
Secrets linger, softly shared,
In the grove, our hearts laid bare.

Misty veils caress the trees,
Echoes dance upon the breeze.
Moonlight drapes in silver shrouds,
Nature speaks in softened crowds.

Every rustle tells a tale,
Of wondrous journeys, love set sail.
Hidden pathways, softly tread,
In twilight's arms, fears are shed.

Fragrant flowers, night's embrace,
Glimmers spark in hidden space.
Memories linger, sweet and bright,
As we wander, hearts take flight.

Evening deepens, stars align,
In this grove, souls intertwine.
Secrets guard like treasures rare,
In twilight's grace, we find our prayer.

Swaying Shadows of Amethyst

In the evening's golden hue,
Swaying shadows dance anew.
Whispers of the night invite,
Hearts awaken in amethyst light.

Petals curl and softly sway,
As twilight bids the sun to play.
Moments spark like falling stars,
In the dusk, our spirit spars.

Hidden paths beneath our feet,
Laughter echoes, bittersweet.
In the weave of night's soft thread,
Dreams unfurl as daylight's shed.

Every sigh a story told,
In the twilight, warm and bold.
Embrace the night, let worries cease,
In swaying shadows, find your peace.

As starlit skies begin to gleam,
Let go of doubts, embrace the dream.
In amethyst waves, we drift away,
In the night's embrace, forever stay.

Dreaming in the Quiet Glade

In whispers soft, the breezes glide,
Amongst the trees, where dreams abide.
Moonlight dances on leaves so bright,
In the stillness of the night.

Stars above, like stories twine,
Each glimmer speaks of hopes divine.
Crickets sing their lullaby sweet,
Where earth and magic gently meet.

A brook meanders, clear and run,
Reflecting dreams beneath the sun.
The air, a canvas, fresh and clear,
Paints visions of what we hold dear.

In this glade, time seems to pause,
Nature whispers, with gentle cause.
In hearts we carry, seeds we sow,
As tranquil breezes softly blow.

With every breath, we weave anew,
Tales of love and skies so blue.
Here, in the quiet, we find our way,
Dreaming deep in the soft light's ray.

The Magic of Hidden Blossoms

In a garden where secrets dwell,
Petals whisper their silent spell.
Colors burst, a vivid sight,
Nature's magic, pure delight.

Each flower holds a story rare,
Beneath the leaves, soft scents declare.
A bloom by chance, a chance to grow,
In hidden nooks where few may go.

Honeybees dance, so sweet and bold,
Gathering tales that must be told.
With gentle wings, they sip and play,
A life of magic in bright display.

As twilight drapes its velvet hue,
The blossoms glow, kissed by dew.
In shadows deep, their beauty beams,
Awakening the night's soft dreams.

So let us wander where they hide,
In nature's arms, let love abide.
For in their grace, we find a way,
To hold the heart of every day.

Weavings of the Night's Embrace

The night unfolds its velvet cloak,
With silver threads, the stars bespoke.
In shadows deep, we find our place,
In whispers soft, the night's embrace.

Moonlight glimmers on the stream,
Carrying forth each gentle dream.
Every echo, a tale untold,
In tranquil silence, hearts unfold.

The owls call with haunting grace,
Guardians of this sacred space.
In the coolness, secrets blend,
Where darkness dances, dreams extend.

Winds weave through the ancient trees,
Carrying scents of the night's breeze.
With every sigh, a story says,
Of whispered hopes and stolen days.

As starlit paths begin to fade,
We cherish all the night has made.
In heart and soul, forever trace,
The woven threads of night's embrace.

Fables of Amethyst and Nightshade

In twilight's grasp, the tales take flight,
Of amethyst dreams and shadowed night.
Whispers carried on the breeze,
Awakening tales beneath the trees.

Nightshade blooms, a mystic guise,
Hiding secrets under starlit skies.
Each petal holds a history grand,
Stories whispered, hand in hand.

The forest hums with ancient lore,
Fables wrapped in nature's core.
With every glance, the heart entreats,
To wander where the mystery meets.

As dreams entwine in cosmic play,
Fables rise to light the way.
Through amethyst shades, we sail,
In reverie, we never fail.

So take my hand, let's drift tonight,
In tales spun from the soft twilight.
With every whisper, rich and deep,
We'll weave the dreams that time will keep.

The Cabal of Whispering Threads

In shadows they gather, silent and bright,
Secrets entwined in the fabric of night.
Soft echoes of laughter, a delicate dance,
Weaving their stories, entranced by the chance.

Threads of intention, they pull and they sew,
Binding their dreams where no one can go.
With whispers like silk, they blend and they weave,
A tapestry spun of what they believe.

Fingers like shadows, they trace every seam,
Embroidering silence, threading a dream.
In the twilight's embrace, conspiracies grow,
The cabal of whispers, with much left to show.

Under the moonlight, their magic ignites,
Crafting illusions with delicate sights.
Together they gather, their spirits aligned,
Woven in darkness, a bond undefined.

As threads intertwine, their secrets ensue,
A cabal of whispers, forever in view.
In the loom of the night, their stories shall thrive,
A union of spirits, eternally alive.

Underneath the Opalescent Veil

Beneath the soft shimmer of moonlit dreams,
A world is unfolding, where nothing seems.
Whispers like breezes, they float and they glide,
Veils worn like shadows, where secrets reside.

Opalescent hues wrap the night in delight,
Guiding the wanderers who seek out the light.
Mysteries linger in starlit embrace,
Hidden reflections, a delicate trace.

In corners of twilight, where echoes converge,
Threads of illusion begin to emerge.
The veil softly drapes over hearts set to roam,
Inviting the lost ones to safely come home.

Stars weave their patterns in the darkened sky,
While dreams intertwine as the moments slip by.
Under the opal veil, time ceases to flee,
A realm full of wonders, forever set free.

As shadows dissolve, and dawn starts to seep,
The veil gently fades, where secrets now sleep.
Yet whispers remain, like a soft melody,
Underneath the surface, forever to be.

Woven Songs of the Night's Garden

In the garden of whispers, beneath the moon's hue,
Songs of the night call to me and to you.
Petals unfurl like soft notes in the breeze,
Woven in silence, with great gentle ease.

Crickets intone in a rhythmic delight,
Nature's sweet chorus, embracing the night.
Stars like soft lanterns, they shimmer and sway,
Guiding the lost on their winding ballet.

The fragrance of jasmine dances on air,
Drawing in dreamers who wander with care.
Each woven song tells a story, a truth,
Echoing softly the essence of youth.

Moonflowers bloom in their ethereal grace,
Casting a glow in this enchanted space.
Whispers entwined in the leaves of the trees,
Sing me a lullaby, sweet like the breeze.

The night's garden thrives in its mysteries known,
And woven songs linger, forever they've grown.
In the hush of the twilight, where shadows confide,
The magic of night will forever abide.

Glistening Beneath the Woven Stars

In twilight's embrace, the stars come alive,
Glistening softly, they flicker and thrive.
Woven together, like threads through the night,
They spark with a glow, casting shadows of light.

Each twinkle a tale from the heavens above,
A message of hope wrapped in wisdom and love.
Glistening whispers cascade through the dark,
Igniting the shadows, igniting a spark.

In silence they shimmer, they dance in delight,
Guiding the dreamers who wander the night.
Under their watch, all the secrets are spun,
Woven in stardust, where journeys begun.

The cosmos, a canvas, where wonders ignite,
Glistening beneath the woven stars' light.
In the heart of the night, mysteries blend,
With stories of worlds that rise and transcend.

So gaze at the heavens, let your spirit soar,
Breathe in the magic, let your heart explore.
For glistening wonders, forever they'll gaze,
Beneath the woven stars, in a shimmering haze.

Dreamweaver's Embrace

In slumber's hold, a gentle sway,
Soft whispers call the night to play.
A tapestry of hopes unspun,
Where dreams and shadows gently run.

Stars glisten like the dew-kissed leaves,
In every heart, a secret weaves.
A dance of light upon the ground,
In fantasy, our souls are found.

Embrace the night, let visions rise,
In stillness, hear the lullabies.
With every sigh, a tale unfolds,
Of brave adventures yet untold.

The moon holds close, a silver thread,
To guide our dreams where we are led.
In this realm, we lose our fears,
And paint our nights with starlit cheers.

So when the dawn begins to break,
Remember all the paths we take.
In waking life, let dreams inspire,
For every heart is a dreamer's fire.

Serenade of the Woven Dusk

As shadows stretch across the land,
The dusk weaves dreams with gentle hand.
A serenade of whispers low,
In twilight's grace, our spirits glow.

Crickets sing, a soft refrain,
While stars emerge, a twinkling chain.
The trees sway with the evening breeze,
In harmony, they dance with ease.

The sky ignites in hues so bright,
Reflecting magic of the night.
With every breath, we find our place,
In woven dusk, a warm embrace.

The world transforms, the colors blend,
In every heart, a chance to mend.
As night unveils its quiet charm,
We seek the light, our spirits arm.

So let us revel in this song,
Where dreams and dusk forever throng.
In twilight's arms, we find our way,
To greet the night, to greet the day.

Dance of the Violet Stalks

In fields adorned with violet hues,
The flowers sway in nature's muse.
A dance of joy beneath the sun,
Where every bloom is freshly spun.

With gentle grace, they bow and rise,
A playful swirl beneath the skies.
Each petal holds a world untold,
A story rich, a memory bold.

The wind sings soft, a tender tune,
As daylight fades and hugs the moon.
Amidst the stalks, the heart takes flight,
In whispers shared with the night.

Each pulse and sway, a lover's beat,
In harmony, our lives repeat.
The violet stalks, they know our dreams,
As moonlight dances with silver beams.

So let us join this meadow's dance,
In every laugh, in every chance.
With nature's pulse, we find our song,
A timeless bond that feels so strong.

Enchanted Twilight Secrets

In twilight's embrace, secrets unfold,
Tales of magic, whispers of old.
Amongst the trees, shadows play,
As dusk invites the stars to sway.

A shimmer glows on paths unseen,
Where light and dark create a sheen.
The moon reveals in softest grace,
A hidden world in this sacred space.

The heartbeats echo in the night,
Where dreams take wing in softest flight.
A tapestry of thoughts divine,
In twilight's arms, our souls entwine.

The air is thick with mystery,
As night unveils its history.
In gentle sighs, we find our fears,
And weave the moments of the years.

Embrace the secrets twilight brings,
In every heartfelt breath, our wings
Will carry hope and love so dear,
As dusk unveils what we hold near.

The Mosaic of Soft Nightfall

Stars gather high in the blanket of night,
Whispers of darkness stir dreams in flight.
Moonbeams drape softly on slumbering trees,
Night's tender brush calms the world's unease.

Crickets sing sweetly their lullabies clear,
The air dances gently, with magic so near.
Shadows embrace, like secrets untold,
In the stillness, night's wonders unfold.

Each petal in silence finds solace so deep,
In the heart of the forest, the twilight's sweep.
Breezes play melodies, starlight ignites,
Painting the cosmos with gentle delights.

Dreams drift like clouds on a sea of dark blue,
Hopes echo softly under soft night's hue.
Cradled by twilight, the world holds its breath,
As magic ensues in the arms of sweet death.

With each passing moment, the night holds her reign,
Crafting a tapestry, echoes of pain.
Yet love still flickers in shadows downcast,
In the mosaic of night, our spirits are cast.

Spheres of Gentle Intrigue

In circles of wonder, the stars intertwine,
Whispers of fate in the threads that they bind.
Mirrors of dreams reflect visions so bright,
Lost in the dance of the cosmos's flight.

Amongst the vast ether, secrets take shape,
Each orbit a story, a chance to escape.
Gentle the pull of magnetic allure,
In realms of intrigue where hearts feel secure.

Orbital wonders, in rhythms compete,
Celestial bodies with mysteries sweet.
Tides of emotion, they ebb and they flow,
Guided by forces we yearn to know.

Colors collide in a sky set ablaze,
Illuminated pathways through cosmic displays.
The pulse of the universe beats ever so free,
In spheres of intrigue, we find our decree.

With each passing moment, the night gently sighs,
Woven in stories as galaxies rise.
A dance of existence, our fates intertwined,
In spheres of gentle intrigue, our souls are aligned.

In the Heart of the Spider's Embrace

Woven with patience, the spider spins fate,
Silken threads shimmering, delicate state.
Every strand tells of the journey she takes,
In the heart of her web, the mystery wakes.

Dewdrops shimmer like diamonds at dawn,
Caught in the gleam of the first light reborn.
In the stillness, the world feels her grace,
In the heart of the spider's embrace.

Time weaves together both joy and despair,
A tapestry rich, both fragile and bare.
Life's fleeting moments are caught in her hold,
A dance of creation, both tender and bold.

With every heartbeat, her art finds its flow,
Mapping the stories of those who don't know.
In shadows she whispers, in light she confides,
In the heart of the spider, the universe hides.

As day softly fades into night's tender sigh,
Each thread we discern holds a truth or a lie.
Embraced by her wisdom, we learn to align,
In the heart of the spider's embrace, we find.

Echoing Colors of Dusk's Whimsy

As the sun dips low, a palette unfurls,
A tapestry painted with hues of the world.
Crimson and gold in a playful ballet,
Whispering secrets that dusk brings our way.

Fluttering shades dance on the edge of the night,
Each moment a brushstroke, alive with delight.
The canvas of skies adorned with soft light,
Echoing stories as day says goodnight.

Twilight ignites all the colors we crave,
A symphony sung by both bold and the brave.
Mingling of shadows, a flourish anew,
In the echoing colors, the spirit breaks through.

The wind carries whispers of dreams yet to dream,
In the heart of the dusk, every spark finds its theme.
As laughter cascades through the branches so free,
Echoes of whimsy shall always be.

With each brush of twilight, we chase fading light,
In the colors of dusk, we felt infinite flight.
A gallery vibrant, where memories play,
In echoing colors, we dance, and we sway.

Echoes of the Enchanted Mist

In the hush where shadows play,
Whispers dance as night turns gray.
Lilies sigh in gentle sweep,
Secrets kept, the world will keep.

Moonlight weaves a silver thread,
Through the dreams that softly spread.
Voices lost within the gloom,
Nature breathes, unfurling bloom.

Mystic fog wraps around the trees,
Holding echoes in the breeze.
Footsteps soft on mossy ground,
In this magic, peace is found.

Every glance holds ancient lore,
In the mist, we seek for more.
Hearts entwined with twilight's glow,
Feel the wonders gently flow.

In the stillness, spirits rise,
Painting dreams across the skies.
Echoes linger, softly kissed,
By the touch of enchanted mist.

The Gentle Touch of Evening

As the sun begins to dip,
Stars awaken, daylight slips.
Crickets hum a lullaby,
While the world lets out a sigh.

Gentle winds through branches sweep,
Bringing whispers from the deep.
Shadows stretch across the land,
Painting dusk with tender hand.

A canvas brushed with hues of gold,
Stories of the day retold.
Clouds like cotton drift and roam,
In this soft and sweetening home.

Night's embrace, a cozy shroud,
Underneath a twilight cloud.
Every heart begins to rest,
Finding comfort, feeling blessed.

In the evening's gentle light,
Hope blooms bright with each new night.
Softly fading, day must yield,
To the dreams that night has sealed.

Twilight's Caress Among the Pines

Among the pines, the twilight calls,
Whispers echo, the shadow falls.
A gentle breeze stirs ancient trees,
As night descends, all worries ease.

Stars ignite in velvet skies,
Painting dreams in lovers' eyes.
Moonbeams dance on forest's floor,
Stirring hearts to seek for more.

Silhouettes in twilight gleam,
Chasing softly, every dream.
Nature breathes with rhythmic ease,
In the hush, the spirit frees.

Fingers trace the bark so rough,
In the quiet, hearts grow tough.
Every sigh, a secret shared,
In this moment, souls laid bare.

Twilight's touch, a tender kiss,
Filling life with quiet bliss.
In the embrace of evening's signs,
We find solace among the pines.

A Symphony of Mist and Bloom

In the morn where colors blend,
Mist rolls softly, dreams transcend.
Petals open, shyly greet,
Nature's symphony, bittersweet.

Morning dew like diamonds shine,
Whispers trace the verdant vine.
On the air, a fragrant tune,
Sung by flowers, kissed by June.

Twisting paths through emerald green,
Where the heart can wander, dream.
In the stillness, magic stirs,
In this place, the spirit purrs.

Waves of color, scents entwine,
Bringing joy, a dance divine.
Every leaf a note on high,
In the breeze, a lullaby.

As the day meets evening's breath,
Life unfolds, embracing death.
In the twilight, softly loom,
A symphony of mist and bloom.

Inhabitant of the Weaving Night

In shadows deep, the whispers sway,
A lone heart drifts, lost in the fray.
Stars embroider the endless dark,
Guiding dreams, igniting a spark.

Moonlight dances on silken threads,
Painting visions where silence spreads.
Ethereal sounds weave through the air,
An inhabitant, lost without care.

The night wraps round like a soft embrace,
Cradling secrets in its vast space.
With each breath, the cosmos sighs,
Awakening souls to the starlit skies.

In the twilight, shadows confide,
A kaleidoscope where hopes abide.
Underneath the celestial dome,
Every heartbeat finds its home.

So linger here, in the weaving night,
Let your spirit take flight, take flight.
With luminous tales, softly guide,
An inhabitant's journey, nowhere to hide.

Mysteries in the Glistening Glow

In the hush of dusk, secrets bloom,
Radiance spills from the twilight gloom.
The air is thick with stories untold,
Wrapped in shadows, glimmering gold.

Nature hums with a soothing sigh,
Beneath the vast, uncharted sky.
Each step leads to a serendipitous fate,
In the glistening glow, we contemplate.

Waves of light dance on silver streams,
Promising more than just fleeting dreams.
Echoes of laughter float on the breeze,
Whispered mysteries weave through the trees.

Moments linger like dew on the grass,
Capturing time as wanderers pass.
With every heartbeat, life colors anew,
In the glistening glow, embrace the view.

So open your eyes to the wonders found,
In the mysteries where dreams abound.
Let your spirit soar, let your heart grow,
In the soft embrace of the glistening glow.

Portraits of the Shimmering Dusk

Framed in hues of fiery red,
The day recedes, while dreams are fed.
Each silhouette holds tales to share,
Of fleeting moments that linger there.

The horizon blurs with whispers of gold,
Timeless stories, moments bold.
Painted skies beckon hearts that yearn,
In the shimmering dusk, passions burn.

Between shadows, where legends lie,
Hopes take flight, destined to fly.
With every breath, a canvas unfolds,
Portraits of life in twilight behold.

The evening sighs with tender grace,
Kissing the stars that softly trace.
In this gallery of the fading light,
Each moment captured, pure and bright.

So linger awhile in dusk's embrace,
Reflect on dreams, find your place.
Where time stands still, let memories rust,
In the portraits of the shimmering dusk.

Spun Dreams in Twilight's Heart

In twilight's heart, where shadows gleam,
Whispers of wishes float like a dream.
Each thread is woven with hope and care,
Spun dreams linger in the cool night air.

Stars awaken in a tapestry grand,
Guiding lost souls with a gentle hand.
The softest glow creates a sacred space,
As hearts align in the serene embrace.

A melody plays on the winds of fate,
Crafting pathways where destinies wait.
With every pulse, the universe calls,
Spun dreams rise as the twilight falls.

In the silence, the world breathes slow,
Painting visions that softly glow.
Time weaves threads of laughter and tears,
Spun dreams cradle our hopes and fears.

So gather your wishes under the stars,
Let them carry you beyond the bars.
In twilight's heart, let your spirit depart,
With spun dreams guiding your inner art.

A Tapestry of Wandering Whispers

In the forest deep, shadows play,
Whispers carry the dreams of day.
Leaves rustle softly, secrets unfold,
Stories of wanderers, ancient and bold.

Mossy paths twist, guide the way,
Footprints linger where dreams sway.
Echoes of laughter, faint and bright,
Dance with the fireflies, holding tight.

Cool breeze beckons, invites the night,
Stars awaken, twinkling light.
Every rustle a tale to tell,
In the tapestry where shadows dwell.

Moonlight paints with silvery grace,
Nature's canvas, a timeless space.
Wandering whispers, soft as sighs,
Weaving magic beneath the skies.

Each step forward, a heartbeat's song,
In this realm where we belong.
A journey crafted of dreams and lore,
In whispers, softly, we explore.

Seraphic Hues in Fading Day

Golden rays spill over the hill,
Time whispers softly, nature stands still.
Crimson and violet, the colors blend,
As daylight bids a gentle end.

Clouds embrace the twilight glow,
A tranquil dance, soft and slow.
Birdsong lingers, a final tune,
Heralding the rise of the silver moon.

Stars emerge as darkness deepens,
Twinkling gems, night's secrets steepen.
Beneath this canvas, hearts align,
In seraphic hues, love intertwines.

Every moment, a brushstroke rare,
Painting dreams in the evening air.
As the sun slips into the west,
Hope ignites, in hearts, a quest.

Fading day, a memory sweet,
In twilight whispers, souls shall meet.
With each breath, the night unfolds,
Wraps us gently in tales untold.

The Allure of the Ethereal Web

In the twilight's hush, shadows weave,
An ethereal web, where dreams believe.
Threads of moonlight, silver and bright,
Stitch together the fabric of night.

Glimmers of hope in the darkest weave,
Whispers of magic, do not deceive.
Every strand holds a story untold,
Of love and loss, of brave and bold.

With every heartbeat, the web expands,
Carried by whispers of unseen hands.
In the stillness, we find our way,
Guided by stars that light our play.

Ethereal beauty glimmers and glows,
In every corner where kindness flows.
Fate's gentle fingers dance and spin,
Inviting us all, the lost and the kin.

Together we weave, our spirits align,
In this web of wonder, a design divine.
The allure of dreams, so deeply spun,
In the heart's fabric, we are one.

Echoing Legends Beneath the Stars

Under the canvas of night, we pause,
To hear the echoes, applause of the stars.
Legends dance on the winds of time,
Whispering tales in rhythm and rhyme.

In the cosmic embrace, myths collide,
Heroes and shadows, side by side.
Each flicker ignites a story anew,
Under the watchful gaze, we imbue.

Constellations draw maps in the sky,
Charting the journeys where dreams can fly.
In the silence, we listen, we learn,
To the echoes of legends that gently churn.

Starlight weaves through the tapestry bright,
Illuminating paths through the darkest night.
With every glance, the past intertwines,
In the heart of the night, our spirit finds.

Beneath the stars, we gather near,
Echoing whispers of love and fear.
Through ages old, our souls do roam,
In the legends shared, we find our home.

Chasing the Soft Gleams

In the quiet of twilight's embrace,
Stars peek out, each a gentle trace.
The moon whispers secrets, soft and bright,
Guiding dreams in the cloak of night.

Rivers hum songs of shimmering light,
While shadows dance, banishing fright.
Each gleam a promise, a fleeting dance,
Awakening hopes in a whispered chance.

Flowers bloom with delicate grace,
Their colors mirror the night's face.
Fleeting moments, like sand through hands,
Drift into dreams, while starlight stands.

Soft winds carry tales of the past,
Echoes of laughter that dimmed too fast.
In the stillness, hearts find their way,
Chasing the soft gleams of yesterday.

So let us wander where wishes roam,
In the embrace of the night we call home.
With every flicker, a heartbeat shared,
Chasing the soft gleams, unprepared.

Interludes of the Spider's Lair

In corners where whispers softly dwell,
Spider spins tales, a mystical spell.
Threads of silver glint in the night,
Holding secrets woven tight.

Little creatures scurry, unaware,
Of the artistry spun with loving care.
An intricate web, both fragile and strong,
Where each silken stitch tells a song.

Raindrops gather, a gentle applause,
For the master who builds with such grace and pause.
In shadows, the dance of nature's art,
An interlude plays, a delicate heart.

Dreams are caught in the fine embrace,
Of dewdrops that hang, a moment's grace.
Life's fleeting journeys, caught up in the thread,
Where whispers of fate and fortune are led.

So in the stillness, let us behold,
The stories of life in webs spun of gold.
Interludes linger, as night turns to dawn,
In the spider's lair, where magic is drawn.

Violets at Dusk's Threshold

Twilight spills colors, soft and rare,
Violets bloom with a fragrant flair.
In the hush of evening, shadows blend,
As daylight slips softly, around the bend.

Petals unfurl, like secrets told,
In whispers of purple, tender and bold.
They sway with the breeze, a gentle sigh,
Welcoming dreams as the light waves goodbye.

The sky, an artist, paints with care,
While violets dance in the cool night air.
Each bloom a promise, a fleeting dream,
At dusk's threshold, they find their gleam.

Beneath the stars, hopes freely rise,
In muted whispers, they touch the skies.
Nature's lullaby cradles the night,
As violets blossom in soft twilight.

So linger awhile in this sacred place,
Where time slows down, and hearts find grace.
Violets at dusk, a sight to see,
A gentle reminder of what can be.

The Tenderness of Whispered Threads

In the quiet corners, where echoes roam,
Whispered threads weave a tapestry home.
Each stitch a heartbeat, a tale retold,
In the warmth of memories, both soft and bold.

Gentle fingers dance with a careful grace,
Binding the moments we cannot replace.
In the strands of love, lose and find,
The tenderness woven within the mind.

Hopes and dreams wrapped snugly tight,
In a symphony played by the stars at night.
Each thread a memory, a joy, or a tear,
An embrace of stories that linger near.

Time slips softly through golden seams,
Intertwining the fabric of our dreams.
With every whisper, a promise stays,
In the tenderness of life's intricate ways.

So treasure the threads, fragile and sweet,
For in their embrace, our journeys meet.
The whispered tales that forever flow,
In the tenderness of love we sew.

Serenity Beneath the Starlit Canopy

Stars twinkle softly in the night,
Whispers of dreams take their flight.
Moonlight dances on the trees,
As the world sighs in gentle ease.

Crickets serenade the calm air,
While shadows form a gentle lair.
Every heartbeat finds its place,
In the stillness, a warm embrace.

The night unfolds a velvet view,
Where secrets glisten, fresh and new.
Underneath this sky so grand,
Hope and wonder go hand in hand.

Breath by breath, the silence grows,
Nature's hush, a soothing prose.
In this haven, cares drift away,
As starlit dreams begin to play.

Held by night, enchanted, free,
Finding peace in harmony.
Serenity wraps us tight,
Beneath the starlit canopy tonight.

Threads of Lilac and Moonlight

Lilac blooms in the twilight's hue,
Whispers of scents that feel so true.
Underneath the silver glow,
Dreams awaken, softly flow.

Each petal glistens, a painted grace,
Carried forth from a secret place.
Moonlight weaves through branches wide,
Guiding footsteps where hopes abide.

Stars are scattered like seeds of light,
In this tapestry of night.
Every thread sings stories bright,
Woven close in pure delight.

Gentle breezes swirl and sway,
Cradle the moment, keep fears at bay.
Through lilac fields, we wander free,
Lost in whispers of eternity.

In this dance of soft embrace,
We find our way, we find our place.
Threads of lilac and moonlight blend,
In nature's arms, our souls transcend.

Echoes in the Gossamer Grove

In the grove where silence sings,
Echoes flutter on fragile wings.
Branches arch in graceful bows,
Embracing secrets, soft as vows.

Misty veils weave through the trees,
Carried gently on the breeze.
Each rustle holds a story old,
Tales of dreams and hearts once bold.

Among the shadows, whispers creep,
As nature holds her breath, asleep.
Glimmers of hope in every glade,
Paint the stillness, never fade.

Underneath the twilight's gaze,
Life unfurls in mystic ways.
Echoes in this sacred space,
A chorus wrapped in pure grace.

In the gossamer, we feel the thread,
Where thoughts and wishes gently spread.
Bound to earth yet reaching high,
In echoes, we learn to fly.

The Aroma of Evening Hues

Evening falls with colors deep,
As every shadow begins to creep.
Aroma swirls on twilight's breath,
Dancing gently, life and death.

Scent of jasmine in the air,
Whispers of night, a sweet affair.
Golden sun slips from the west,
Painting dreams as we lay to rest.

With lavender kisses on the breeze,
Every moment meant to please.
The horizon bleeds shades of blue,
As the sky wraps us in its hue.

Dusk unfolds her silken shroud,
A world transformed, soft and proud.
Embracing all with tender grace,
In this quiet, we find our place.

In the aroma of evening views,
Hearts compose their gentle muse.
In every breath, a story begins,
As night descends, and daylight thins.

Elysian Threads of Dusk

In twilight's soft embrace, we weave,
The whispers of the night, we cleave.
Starlit dreams, on shadows prance,
As dusk descends, we seize the chance.

With each thread, the colors blend,
Nature's hand, a gentle mend.
Golden hues and silver sighs,
In elysian light, our spirit flies.

The breeze carries tales so sweet,
Where earth and sky, in twilight meet.
A tapestry of peace unfolds,
As dusk wraps us in its folds.

Crickets serenade the night,
While fireflies dance, a fleeting light.
In the silence, secrets lay,
Elysian threads, in soft decay.

So linger here, as day departs,
With dusk's embrace, create new starts.
For in this hour, all dreams align,
In threads of dusk, we intertwine.

The Webbed Mystique of the Violet Wild

In violet fields where shadows blend,
Each petal tells a tale, no end.
Webbed mysteries in every hue,
As nature crafts her art anew.

The wind whispers of secrets untold,
In the heart of wilds, brave and bold.
Where twilight dances on a whim,
In violet embrace, the world grows dim.

A symphony of colors in flight,
In webs of magic, pure delight.
Each blossom, a note of sweet refrain,
As stars awaken, the wild remains.

Dew-kissed dreams at dawn's first light,
With hopes entwined in the soft night.
Violet wonders, a tender hold,
In mystique's grasp, our hearts unfold.

So wander deep, where silence calls,
In the violet wild, where the spirit enthralls.
For within each thread of nature's weave,
A webbed enchantment, we believe.

Moonlit Petals in the Glade

In glades where moonlight softly streams,
Petals unfurl, revealing dreams.
A silver cloak on nature's floor,
Where heartbeats echo, and spirits soar.

The tranquil night, a whispered song,
With fragrant blooms, we drift along.
Each step reveals a world anew,
Beneath the gaze of the stars' soft hue.

The stillness cradles ancient lore,
In every petal, we explore.
The moonlit path, a guiding light,
In glades of magic, we unite.

With shadows dancing, time stands still,
As petals open to the thrill.
The night unfolds its sweet embrace,
In moonlit glade, we find our place.

So let us roam through dreams we share,
In nature's peace, a love laid bare.
For in the petals' gentle sighs,
Moonlit whispers, where magic lies.

Harmonies of the Silken Silhouettes

In twilight's glow, silhouettes sway,
In nature's harmony, they play.
Silken forms in the fading light,
Whisper secrets of the night.

With every breath, the shadows hum,
A melody of where dreams come.
In whispers soft, the world aligns,
In silken grace, our souls entwine.

The rustling leaves, a tender score,
In quiet moments, we explore.
Each silhouette, a story told,
In harmonies of dusk, unfold.

The stars above, like echoes gleam,
Illuminate the night's grand dream.
In the dance of light and shade,
Harmonies in silence are laid.

So let us linger in this art,
Where nature's tunes embrace the heart.
In silken forms, we find our way,
In harmonies that softly sway.

Starlit Secrets in Winged Worlds

In the hush of night's embrace,
Secrets whisper, taking flight.
Stars above weave tales so bright,
Guiding dreams through endless space.

Feathers brush against the sky,
As echoes of the past resound.
Each twinkle, a forgotten cry,
In winged worlds, wonders abound.

Moonlit pathways twist and turn,
Unraveling threads of ancient lore.
In shadows where the fireflies yearn,
Starlit secrets, forevermore.

Beneath the canvas, dreams compile,
Painting hopes with silken grace.
Each heartbeat marks a fleeting mile,
In the realms of the ethereal space.

Awakening to dawn's soft glow,
The stories linger in the air.
Through the branches, whispers flow,
In winged worlds, we're everywhere.

A Dance with the Shadowed Garden

In the twilight's soft embrace,
Shadows swirl, a gentle waltz.
Petals fall, a fleeting grace,
In the garden where silence halts.

Moonbeams filter through the leaves,
Casting spells of silver light.
Where the heartache gently weaves,
The shadow dances with delight.

Secrets bloom in every corner,
Whispers hush in fragrant night.
Each flower wakes, a silent mourner,
In the garden of lost delight.

Footsteps weave with tender care,
A melody of hope and pain.
In the shadows, dreams lay bare,
Echoes of love's sweet refrain.

With the dawn, the dance will cease,
Yet memories linger, soft and sweet.
In the garden, find your peace,
In shadowed realms, our hearts repeat.

Allure of the Woven Wilds

In the forest where echoes call,
Woven wilds of nature's thread.
Mysteries hide where shadows fall,
Dance of whispers, softly said.

Crimson leaves and emerald vines,
Intertwined in a tapestry.
Every heartbeat softly shines,
In the wilds, we are set free.

Beneath the boughs, the secrets weave,
Stories of lives once intertwined.
In every rustle, dreams believe,
In the wilds, fate is unconfined.

A chorus sung by the unseen,
Nature's song, a guiding star.
Where the heart ignites the glean,
In woven paths, we wander far.

Through the thickets, hope will bloom,
In the land where time stands still.
Amidst the wilds, dispel all gloom,
For in their grasp, our spirits thrill.

Threads of Elysian Mystery

In the realm where dreams entwine,
Threads of fate weave stories bold.
Whispers float on night's design,
Timeless tales waiting to unfold.

Elysian skies in pastel hues,
Hold the secrets of the past.
With every glance, a spark imbues,
A mystery that's meant to last.

Stars descend like silken strands,
Stitching moments to our hearts.
In the darkness, destiny stands,
As the dance of life departs.

Through the tapestry of night,
We wander, lost yet found.
Each thread spun with pure delight,
In this ether, love unbound.

As dawn approaches, shadows fade,
Yet the echoes softly stay.
In Elysian dreams we wade,
Threads of mystery lead the way.